BETTER BITCOINING

G̲ET IT RIGHT THE FIRST TIME.
A̲VOID BEING SCAMMED.

BETTER BITCOINING

GET IT RIGHT THE FIRST TIME.
AVOID BEING SCAMMED.

By
S. Roze

Copyright 2018 S. Roze

Publishing Services by Happy Self Publishing
www.happyselfpublishing.com

All rights reserved. No part of this publication may be reproduced, distributed, or transmitted in any form or by any means, including photocopying, recording, or other electronic or mechanical methods, without the prior written permission of the publisher, except in the case of brief quotations embodied in reviews and certain other non-commercial uses permitted by copyright law.

Dedication

This book is dedicated to my sons
Joseph Hobbs, Ahdir Hobbs, and
to my daughter Anyrhee Hobbs.
This book is also dedicated to the many
teachers I have had along the way.

Table of Contents

Acknowledgments 9

Introduction 11

Chapter 1: What is Cryptocurrency? 15

Chapter 2: Popular types of cryptocurrency 21

Chapter 3: Basics of manual mining for profit ... 29

Chapter 4: Basics of cloud mining for profit 45

Chapter 5: Mining pools and what to mine 53

Chapter 6: Getting in the game, getting
a wallet; no sweat 63

Chapter 7: Time to buy Bitcoin off-chain
and mainstream methods 71

Chapter 8: Converting currencies 87

Chapter 9: Don't get burned out there 93

References: 105

Glossary 109

About the Author 115

Acknowledgments

This book could not have been possible without the love and support of my friends and closest family members. Thank you to everyone who agreed to read early editions of the book.

BETTER BITCOINING-
DON'T BE A VICTIM

Introduction

Have you heard of cryptocurrency? Would you like to know more about it, but are you scared to even think about losing your hard-earned money? I was too. Are you not investor savvy at all? This book is written for people not familiar with financial market trading. Also, maybe you don't even care about the new digital money. Well, that's not going to make the new money go away. Cryptocurrency is here to stay. So, why not just get your hands on some of it already?

After reading "Better Bitcoining," you will be able to talk intelligently about basic cryptocurrency anywhere you go. You will learn the basic meat and potatoes of the cryptocurrency world and its lingo. If you choose, you can also set up a digital currency wallet, and buy your first Bitcoin shares or alternate coin shares right from your hand device or a device of your choice.

This book was written to show you some not so obvious ways to avoid losing your money as you are getting started in the exciting digital currency world. I personally lost over three thousand dollars. This does not have to be your story. I also now make consistent money with digital currency. You need to know the simple ways you can do the same.

Each chapter gives some short, information-packed data that is easy to digest relating to the core terms and topics surrounding the new digital currency market. Each chapter leaves you feeling well versed and certainly abreast of the latest topic that is on everyone's lips. You might even start making money to back up your newfound knowledge.

We will start by easing into the information so that you know each term by the time you get to setting up your wallet. By the end of this book, you will know exactly what you're doing, and you'll be able to tell and show all your friends how smart you have become. Having some money to prove it will be nice too.

Let's get started!

CHAPTER I

What is Cryptocurrency?

Cryptocurrency is the newest form of money. Yes, the name crypto "currency" probably gave you a pretty good idea that it's money. However, this is not paper money. It's digital money. As opposed to our current fiat currencies such as the US dollar, yen, euro etc., cryptocurrency is a new decentralized form of currency that the world is quickly adopting. The need for a new medium of exchange other than paper money has been looming over our heads for over a century now. We should not be surprised to see the wide acceptance of a new currency.

Cryptocurrency is made by verifying pervious transactions of the same type of cryptocurrency in a batch on a blockchain. A blockchain is a form of public ledger or public transaction record that can be seen by anyone. Inside each batch on the blockchain, there will be a variable number of confirmations required by different miners at various locations around the world to verify the accuracy of that particular cryptocurrency transaction. The verified transaction can then be traced back to that blockchain batch transaction forever. Each type of cryptocurrency is verified using a specific algorithm. This algorithm is a sort of cryptographic puzzle specific to that currency. Each time a prior transaction is verified by the cryptocurrency using the assigned algorithm, a new fraction of a unit of that specific kind of cryptocurrency is created. Each of these fractions of units of that particular cryptocurrency will add up to a whole unit or, what we call, a single coin. So you might be thinking where digital currency came from? Well, there are a few stories circulating out there.

As early as 1998, the concept of cryptocurrency was described in a mailing list called

Cypherpunks by a man named Wei Dai.[1] It was then that Wei Dai began suggesting a new type of money that uses cryptography. What is cryptography? Cryptography is the science or study of the techniques of secret writing especially code and cipher systems, methods, and the like.

Wei Dai suggested using cryptography as opposed to using a central regulated authority to create and control money creation.

Other pioneers in cryptocurrency include David Chaun who first introduced ecash protocols. Along the same lines were Stefan Brands and Alan Back who developed and introduced hashcash. Hashcash was a proof of work scheme for controlling spam within the blockchains. Ultimately, it would be Wei Dai's b-money and Nick Szabo's bitgold together with Hal Finney's reusable proof of work protocols that would propel the digital currency craze forward.

Only some eleven years later did the cryptography concept get proven. The first

---

1 McAllister, Olivia. "Bitcoin Is the First Implementation of a Concept Called "cry." Prezi.com. November 03, 2013. Accessed January 13, 2018. https://prezi.com/3er5jl_ceim-/bitcoin-is-the-first-implementation-of-a-concept-called-cry/.

actual proof of concept through proof of work of cryptography resulting in a blockchain specification was published in 2009.[2] In this cryptography mailing list, a man named Satoshi Nakamoto introduced a coin called Bitcoin. The Bitcoin protocol and software was introduced to the world by Satoshi Nakamoto and was published openly for any developer to review or modify. In 2010, Nakamoto left the Bitcoin development project. Since Satoshi left the project, there have been many developers and many modifications made to the Bitcoin network.

Cryptocurrency gained increasing trust from customers and merchants alike over the last eight years. There are a number of reasons why cryptocurrency has gained so much trust. Cryptocurrency offers transparency and predictability in payment transactions. This just really means that no individual or organization can manipulate the cryptocurrency protocols because they are protected by cryptography. Users are fully protected because merchants cannot force unwanted charges through to wallets.

---

2 Ding, Quan."Ethereum/wiki."GitHub. Accessed February 15, 2018. https://github.com/ethereum/wiki/wiki/White-Paper.

Also, personal and sensitive data are protected during transactions due to the use of only wallet addresses to complete transactions. This key factor is attractive because it protects against identity theft. This key factor also allows merchants to expand into territories where extreme credit card fraud existed in the past. Cryptocurrency now allows merchants to accept secure forms of payment for goods and services in these high-risk markets.

Cryptocurrency transaction fees are another attractive user perk. Fees associated with cryptocurrency transactions vary and can be chosen by the user. Users have an option to choose lower or higher transaction fees based on how fast they want their transaction processed. Cryptocurrency, overall, gives users more control over their currency transactions, and the fees that are paid for completing those transactions.

CHAPTER 2

Popular types of cryptocurrency

Bitcoin

The Bitcoin (BTC) that was introduced by Satoshi Nakamoto in 2009 is the first digital currency with the highest market value to date.[3] With that being said, ask anyone who has lost all their money when bitcoin took a dive, and they might argue that Bitcoin (BTC) is also the worst performing cryptocurrency experience they have had. During the writing of this book, Bitcoin price is currently $6,700.00, down some

---

3 Crowder, David. "Top 10 Best Cryptocurrency List by Performance and Market Capitalization in 2017." Top 10 Best Cryptocurrencies List in 2017. September 11, 2017. Accessed January 12, 2018. https://www.mineweb.net/top-10-cryptocurrency-list.

$13,000.00 from Bitcoin's all time high price of $19,783.06 in December 2017.[4]

Bitcoin is an intangible representation of a digital currency. You cannot physically hold a Bitcoin in your hand. What you hold as a Bitcoin owner is more like a percentage representation of a share or shares on the Bitcoin network. The Bitcoin percentage share was created by someone mining on the Bitcoin network. Mining Bitcoin is the only way to create Bitcoin. Mining is adding a transaction to the public Bitcoin ledger. Think back to what we discussed about cryptography. Bitcoin was created with a proof of work algorithm that can be duplicated repeatedly in a public permanent ledger. Each time a Bitcoin transaction is confirmed; a percentage of a Bitcoin is created and distributed to the owners associated with that Bitcoin transaction confirmation. You only get paid Bitcoin if you mine it yourself, buy it, or it is given to you. The total coin creation for Bitcoin as set by Bitcoin software developers is 21 million coins. That is the total Bitcoin (coins) that developers want to create.

---

4 Morris, David Z. "Bitcoin Hits a New Record High, But Stops Short of $20,000." Fortune. December 17, 2017. Accessed January 12, 2018. http://fortune.com/2017/12/17/bitcoin-record-high-short-of-20000/.

Bitcoin is an open and public network. What this means is that no one individual or organization owns Bitcoin. Bitcoin operates on a consensus system where all owners must comply and agree with developments in order for the Bitcoin network to sustain its value. All owners must use the same software complying with the same rules. The current Bitcoin compliant algorithm running is called Sha-256. This is only relevant if the users on the network are actually mining. This book will *not* discuss technical terms. We will only discuss terms you will actually use often in your transactions with cryptocurrency.

Bitcoin had previously been fully unchecked and regulated by fiat currency regulating bodies. Between 2016 and 2017, the demand for mining Bitcoin and owning Bitcoin quickly became a prestige statement and a social status qualifier for assumed quick wealth. The Bitcoin price continued to increase reaching gains over 1000 percent for many regular, non-investor savvy people. The extreme demand for the digital new currency helped skyrocket public faith in it. By September 2016, the number of Bitcoin ATMs had doubled over an eighteen-month period and had reached seven hundred and seventy-one Bitcoin ATMs worldwide.[5]

Clearly, by the end of 2016 and early 2017, we began to see more and more end users including merchants using and accepting the new digital currency as means of exchange for goods and services. In January 2017, the Japanese Broadcasting Corporation reported that the number of online stores accepting Bitcoin in Japan had increased 4.6 times since 2016.[6] Multiple American giant corporations were not far behind.

What are alternate coins?

In 2014, there were four hundred and seventy-eight altcoins on the crypto market. Alternate cryptocurrency is digital money coins that are currently in circulation. It is any digital currency similar to but not the Bitcoin. Therefore, it is an alternate currency or coin to Bitcoin. So, again, alternate coins describe every cryptocurrency that is not Bitcoin. Each altcoin hopes to

---

5 (47), Ansarmehmood, Cheetah (73), and Coin.info (42)."Bitcoin Growth.- Steemit."- Steemit.Accessed January 16, 2018. https://steemit.com/bitcoin/@ansarmehmood/bitcoin-growth.
6 Bitcoin-made-easy.com. "About Bitcoin." Bitcoin Made Easy. Accessed January 05, 2018. https://bitcoin-made-easy.com/about-bitcoin/.

improve upon or replace Bitcoin. All coins use the same building blocks as Bitcoin, but different algorithmic scripts are used to confirm transactions. The new confirmed transactions, like with Bitcoin, will also create new coins or new currency inside that particular alternate coin.

The first alternate coin created was called the Namecoin. Though this is a currency, the focus of Namecoin was to decentralize the online identities of online users. This book will not focus on Namecoin as this book is focused on currency coins. However, it is worth mentioning the Namecoin as it was the first altcoin.

Litecoin

Litecoin is one of the first top altcoins that performed good enough to call itself the silver to the Bitcoin gold. Litecoin is the third oldest cryptocurrency, and it is the eighth largest capitalized cryptocurrency with its cap at $81 million dollars.[7] Litecoin has increased in value over 7000 percent compared to Bitcoin increase, which was only over 1000 percent in

---

7 Wikipedia."List of Cryptocurrencies."WikiVividly.Accessed February 16, 2018.
https://wikivividly.com/wiki/List_of_cryptocurrencies.

the past year. Litecoin was created by Charles Lee, a former Google engineer. Mr. Lee created Litecoin to be faster than Bitcoin in processing time. Charles Lee left Litecoin in 2017 amid accusations that his comments on Twitter influenced the coin too much.[8]

Although Litecoin is a clone of Bitcoin, it uses a different algorithm to process transactions. Like all cryptocurrencies, Litecoin is created by public miners who confirm previous Litecoin transactions. Litecoin was created so that anyone could mine it easily. The Scrypt algorithm used by Litecoin makes it a faster processing software confirming transactions in 2.5 minutes versus Bitcoin's 10 minutes. Litecoin has been considered useful for smaller digital currency purchases. Litecoin reached a fork on Sunday, February 18, 2018. Litecoin split into Litecoin cash. Litecoin cash is the newest digital currency resulting from the fork in the original Litecoin digital currency.

---

8 McQuaid, Darius. "Litecoin Founder DUMPS Personal Stash to Avoid CONFLICT of Interests." Express.co.uk. December 20, 2017. Accessed February 13, 2018.
https://www.express.co.uk/finance/city/894657/litecoin-Charlie-Lee-bitcoin-fork.

Ethereum

Ethereum went live on July 30, 2015 starting with 11.5 million coins.[9] Ethereum is a currency, but it is also a decentralized application platform. Ethereum is a stable platform that has undergone several protocol upgrades. Its platform is the best one available for smart contract developers. Ethereum supports a modified version of Nakamoto's consensus. Decentralized application platforms are called DAPPs. DAPPs can be run without human intervention once the algorithm is set. DAPPs fail at the human programming stage where the highest chance of error occurs. Any program is only as good as the human programming it. Other software and programs are built on Ethereum's platform because it is a DAPP. Bitcoin runs on a DAPP as well. The value of Ethereum grew over 13,000 percent in 2017.[10] The same year, Ethereum split into two separate blockchains. This caused Ethereum to become Ethereum and Ethereum Classic.

---

9 Palmer, Daniel. "Who Created Ethereum?" CoinDesk. March 30, 2017. Accessed February 20, 2018.
https://www.coindesk.com/information/who-created-ethereum/.
10 Kharpal, Arjun. "Ethereum Hits a Fresh Record High and Is up over 13,000% in a Year." CNBC. January 10, 2018. Accessed February 21, 2018. https://www.cnbc.com/2018/01/10/ethereum-price-hits-record-high-above-1400-up-17000-percent-in-a-year.html.

Fork digital currencies

Bitcoin Cash, Litecoin Cash, and Ethereum Classic are all digital currencies that resulted from a fork in the original digital currencies. A fork is a change or an upgrade to a digital currency software significant enough to create two separate versions of the blockchain. A fork can be temporary for a few minutes or permanent. The forks in Bitcoin, Ethereum, and Litecoin are permanent. Forks allow the software to be improved over time. The improvements need to be agreed upon and supported by the other digital currency supporters and developers for it to take place. Coinbase currently only supports one forked cryptocurrency. That is Bitcoin Cash.

CHAPTER 3

Basics of manual mining for profit

Bitcoin is now traded on the stock exchange. This book will not cover trading on the open financial markets. This book is written for people not familiar with financial market trading. The types of moneymaking we will discuss, for the most part, will involve mining the cryptocurrency.

Mining cryptocurrency

Mining cryptocurrency can be done in a cloud, manually, or individually from a physical location. Mining will cost some money whether it is just the electricity that you will use for your PC or laptop mining. What is mining of cryptocurrency? Mining any cryptocurrency will require you to use your hardware and applicable software to confirm prior transactions executed within that particular digital currency platform. Therefore, if you are going to mine Bitcoins, you will need to have the correct mining software and hardware to solve Bitcoin algorithms. How fast your software and hardware can confirm these transactions, using your own electricity, will determine how fast you can make or mine the Bitcoin currency.

Manual mining requirements

Mining covers three core agendas. First, mining provides a twenty-four hour accounting system to the cryptocurrency you are mining. You will be taking part in this. Don't worry; you don't have to be an accountant to do mining. Remember, mining is your computer solving a specific algorithm to verify prior transactions on the blockchain. Second, mining seeks to compensate each miner for his or her use of resources and time by rewarding the miner with a percentage of currency for his or her services. Third, although not any less important, is keeping your costs to a minimum while mining. These costs will include hardware and electricity costs.

This is very important in fact, because the lesser your costs the more profit you make from mining.

There are a number of essential items you will need to successfully mine cryptocurrency from your home. I will discuss the following requirements briefly.

- First, *you will need a desire to learn more as you make money in cryptocurrency.* You will always have to read and lookout for new information on mining. Always be on the lookout for ways to save on electricity as well. You must be willing to spend the time to find ways to adjust and improve your mining equipment.

Next, we will look at the hardware required to make money through home mining.

- *You will need a personal computer.* The best miners have had their personal computers customized to their mining requirements. There is simply not enough money to be made for people to invest time and energy mining from a mobile device or a laptop. So, I wouldn't waste my time. If you decide to use your current desktop to mine cryptocurrency, you will not be able to use the desktop for any other purpose while you are mining.

- *You will need a digital wallet.* Other names for this could be coin wallet or a network ledger. This digital wallet functions like your physical wallet except it is virtual. Do not let the virtual idea take away from the fact that the fiat currencies you will transfer this digital money into is, in fact, very real and spendable. Your digital wallet is actually a software program. This program stores private and public cryptography keys and is able to interact with different blockchains. This gives the software ability to add and subtract from your balance and report converted currency balances in your digital wallet. Remember, your digital currency balances do not reflect tangible coins. We discussed earlier about your digital currency representing shares of the digital currency. These shares only become tangible when you decide to convert the digital currency into tangible fiat currency. We will discuss in depth about the types of wallets and getting your wallet set up in a later chapter.

- *You will need a Graphics Processing Unit (GPU) or ASICs mining chip.* The graphics processing unit or application-specific integrated circuit provides the accounting work and the horsepower required to do the mining of cryptocurrency. A GPU is one of the two ways to do manual mining that we will discuss here. GPUs do not run on their own. They must be configured to a rig and cannot be used right out of the box. GPUs are the same size as ASICs, but they require more than one unit to earn a profit. They are also complicated to configure and set up. Unlike ASICs, GPUs can be configured to mine multiple coins. The coins that GPUs mine are the coins that ASICs do not mine. These coins are generally worth much less than Bitcoin.

Building a good GPU rig is costly because it takes a number of different components to complete a rig. A rig is a self-contained compartment that is usually held together by some kind of casing, which holds all of your GPUs in one place. They are run and cooled in the container housing them. The rig consists of the casing and the GPUs combined in one unit. Some rigs come with every part included; in other rigs, you will have to add parts. It is because GPUs do not run on their own that this set up is so costly. You will need at least five or six of these units in a rig to earn a profit on mining. The GPUs are easily purchased at local stores and online. That is because these units are popular gaming cards as well. That is one of the upsides of mining with GPUs. Generally, there will not be inflation in price or shortage of cards like you will find with the ASICs units. However, it is reported that it will take you six months or more to get your return on your investment. That is because GPUs provide a low daily profit per single unit. Each unit can only earn about three to four dollars a day. This is why rigs are stacked with multiple units. Good miners have multiple rigs running. Once you have earned back the return on your investment, all the money these rigs make is profit until mining is no longer profitable. It is important to point out that GPUs have great resale value at a minimum of fifty percent of the initial cost. This is one of the advantages of mining with these units. Considering most rigs will cost between $2500 and $6000 to build, getting half of that money back doesn't sound too bad.

ASIC miners are another way to manually mine. ASICs provide three times more profit from mining than GPUs. ASICs also produce more heat and noise than general processing units do. Moreover, these application-specific integrated circuits are only profitable if they are purchased at the original price. The wait time to purchase an application-specific integrated circuit at original price can be numerous weeks or months considering shipping time during high demand periods. Application-specific integrated circuits are programmed to mine only certain algorithms. They provide proof of work faster than general processing units do. Application-specific integrated circuits are noisy units and require a separate dedicated room in order to mine from them. There are application-specific integrated circuits that can mine more than one algorithm, but they are generally designed to mine one coin. Application-specific integrated circuit units are easy to use, and they offer no setup hassles unlike general processing units. These units can be plugged in and operated directly out of the box with very little to no setup. ASICs have higher hash rates than GPUs, which means they calculate problems faster than general processing units do. The downside of mining with ASICs is that there is very little resale value in the event that mining a specific currency becomes unprofitable in the future. Application-specific integrated circuits are less costly to mine with at start-up compared to mining with GPUs. This is because GPUs require additional general processing units, usually up to six or more inside a rig coupled with a PC, in order to mine cryptocurrency. ASICs do not require additional units in order to mine cryptocurrency; they operate solely and independently on their own. The top earning application-specific integrated circuits today will cost around $2000.00 and depending on the Bitcoin price, will earn a minimum of around $300.00 per month. It is quite easy to see how you can gain your return on investment using the application-specific integrated circuits much faster than using a general processing unit to mine your cryptocurrency. In most cases, your return on investment after purchasing an ASIC unit will take between three and six months depending on the Bitcoin price fluctuation. Any monies earned after that time period is all profit after deducting your electricity cost, of course.

- *You will need access to and the knowledge of how online currency exchanges work.* Online currency exchanges are just that. They are virtually digital. You probably can travel to one of these physical locations to do your transactions, but this will be very time consuming. Online currency exchanges charge various fee amounts depending on how fast you want your transaction to be processed. These exchanges will convert your currency from one form to another form in a matter of seconds or hours depending on the transaction fee chosen for your confirmation by the miners. You are essentially paying miners fees when you pay transaction fees to convert your currency. On these online currency exchanges, you can convert both fiat and cryptocurrencies back and forth. Make sure you do your research on the online currency exchange you intend to use. Although, generally, they will all function the same, you will need to know how to use online currency exchanges. You will want to know how to convert fiat currency (e.g. dollars, Euros, pounds, yen etc.) to the digital currency that you are interested in working with. The reverse conversion knowledge is also required for your calculations when you are cashing out your digital currency to fiat currency. Prior online conversions can be completed by you ahead of time and greatly simplified with a simple Google search for online currency conversion.

You can simply type, "Convert Bitcoin to US dollars" into the Google search bar. All your online currency converters will appear. During this step, you will want to pay close attention to the decimal point and the number of zeros you are entering into the input boxes to get a correct currency conversion value.

- For example, Bitcoin uses at least eight to ten zeros in its cryptocurrency valuation to get to it US dollar conversion value. Simply forgetting one zero can result in a higher or lower cryptocurrency conversion value. Cryptocurrency users like online exchanges because your financial transactions can be completed in a matter of minutes or even seconds depending on the currency you are working with. All this can be done without leaving the comfort of your home. Again, pay close attention to the amount of fees each exchange charges for converting the currency you are interested in working with. Each online exchange has different transaction fees. You will want to choose the exchange with the lowest transaction fees relative to your desired transaction processing time.

- *You will need a stable, strong Internet connection.* An Internet connection will not be necessary to mine in a cloud with the large mining farms like Genesis Mining and Hashflare Mining. You will need to maintain a good Internet connection if you are going to mine with the cloud mining company NiceHash. The same will be true for NiceHash Mining if you are a seller of hashing rate. Remember, that only means that you own mining hardware and want to rent it out online to buyers of hashing rate. You will rent your hashing power to the highest bidder on NiceHash. A strong and stable Internet connection is going to be necessary for both GPU mining and ASIC unit mining. Most internets are available with broadband connection of at least 3G, so this is good. 4G and 5G speeds work optimally as well. Also, note that you can mine with DSL Internet connection. However, you will experience latency problems. Latency is when your pool is operating faster than your equipment, and you are not calculating at the same rate that other miners in your pool are calculating algorithms. You want reliable Internet because latency causes reduced profits. It means your mining equipment is lagging, and your hashing rate is slowing down. So keep in mind how important a stable Internet connection is going to be for mining your cryptocurrency.

- *You will need knowledge of mining pools and the ability to join mining pools.*

    What is a mining pool? Every coin that can be mined today has a number of mining pools supported by other miners mining that same coin. It is a community or group of fellow miners like you that want to mine a particular coin. The members of any mining pool will combine their computers together in the mining pool. This combination of computers together in a pool increases the profitability of the pool, and it makes the coin payouts stable within that mining pool. Some mining pools operate better and yield higher profits than others yield. Mining pools operate online. If you are mining with your own hardware, and you join a mining pool, you have become a seller of your hash rate. If you do not own your own hardware for mining, you will join a mining pool as a buyer of hash rate. You will need to know where to find information about the coin that you are mining, and where those pools are. Finding the best mining pool to join can be as easy as doing a Google search on the best mining pool for your coin—the one you are interested in mining. You can then copy and paste the pool selections into the required location, as needed, when placing your mining orders on the respective mining sites.

- *You will need a dedicated place to run your hardware.*

    To be clear, mining at home *is not* recommended for apartments. The noise the units generate is just too loud to be run out of an apartment. Both GPUs and Application-Specific ASIC units generate a lot of heat when performing calculations. Finding the right location to mine your cryptocurrency is key to keeping your mining operation running smoothly. Spare rooms, garages, basements, and sheds are good options for mining at home locations. These are the best location recommendations since the noise and heat is something you must take into consideration when choosing a mining location in your home. Some miner's find that if their mining hardware is positioned correctly after taking the noise into consideration, the heat that is generated from the running units can heat a portion of their house if not their entire house because heat rises.

- *You will need house fans.*

    Since running mining equipment in your home generates so much heat, you will be required to at least use a house fan. The more mining equipment you decide to run, the larger and more powerful fans you will need. A house fan can be used in a window like an exhaust, which blows outward to remove the heat from the area you were mining in. House fans can also be used to blow cool air directly onto the mining units. Your ability to keep the mining equipment cool will be an essential part of running a successful mining operation.

- *You will need free online mining software.*

Why do you need mining software? You need it because this software contains the cryptography for the algorithm your coin is to mine with. Without the appropriate mining software, you will not have any success mining your desired coin. For instance, you cannot mine Ethereum cryptocurrency using Bitcoin cryptocurrency software. Free mining software downloads are available with the hardware that you purchase to mine cryptocurrency. Other free mining software is available online with a simple Google search. You will need to download the software onto your PC in order to mine any cryptocurrency.

CHAPTER 4

Basics of cloud mining for profit

At first glance, setting up to cloud mine cryptocurrency can be very intimidating. This is especially true if you do not follow along well with reading in between the lines during online, audio, and video presentations. It is going to be helpful for you to have a reference place to go back to during your setup process. Cloud mining is renting your hashing rate from another party apart from yourself for a fee in addition to any transaction fees. You will rent this hashing rate from another party because you don't have the money to invest in all the hardware yourself. You will also rent hash rate from another party because you don't know how to configure all the necessary components required to run an at-home mining operation. Renting hash rate from another party via cloud mining allows you to make profits from helping in the mining process of particular coins without investing thousands of dollars upfront for hardware and software setups to run at home.

Cloud mining providers and requirements

There are quite a few cloud mining alternatives available. The top cloud mining providers are Genesis Mining, Hashflare Mining, and NiceHash Mining.

If you are a buyer of hash power, you will use these available online sites to rent power to mine your coins. If you are a seller of hash rate, you will use cloud mining to make your hardware available during its downtime to the highest bidder for the use of your hash rate power. A seller of hashing power can also dedicate its hardware to be used twenty-four hours a day to mine cryptocurrency. Initially, when cloud mining contracts came out, they were for the duration of a lifetime. Anyone can see how such a contract may not be profitable to a corporation. Of course, as buyers, we would be extremely happy with a deal like this. Today, if I could spend one thousand dollars in investment funds and receive my return on investment in one hundred eighty days, I would be happy. I would be even happier if I could continue to get one thousand dollars every one hundred and eighty days for the rest of my life without investing any other money. To date, as far as I know, lifetime mining contracts do not exist anymore. All those contracts have been converted by the company owners to time expiring contracts. Of the available cloud mining options, Genesis Mining and Hashflare Mining are actually very large farm mining corporations. These two companies are your best choices for safe online cloud mining. These mining companies require that you lock your money up for a minimum time, usually a year. NiceHash allows shorter mining contracts than both Genesis Mining and Hashflare Mining. With the current volatility in cryptocurrency values, it may be beneficial to mine in small amounts of time and in small amounts when just getting your feet wet in mining. Cloud mining in small amounts of time allows you to catch upswings in mining profitability and coin values. This also allows you to get out quickly if coin values and mining profitability begin to drop for the cryptocurrency you are mining. It is important to note that some people may even compare mining cryptocurrency to gambling as opposed to likening it to any real form of investment. Although there is real spendable money to be made from mining cryptocurrency, it is not made overnight. There is no cloud mining venture that will yield a get rich quick result. All the rewards for cloud mining are paid out evenly to the number of participants in the mining pool mining a particular block. The timing of the payout is set within the algorithm. Bitcoin pays the slowest right now at every ten minutes.

Also, worth taking a closer look at is the cloud mining platform of NiceHash. NiceHash cloud mining is different from the other cloud mining platforms in that it functions more like a brokerage service. It is the middleman between buyers who want to rent hashing power and individual sellers who want to rent out their rigs either twenty-four hours a day or just during their computer downtime. The NiceHash mining platform allows buyers and sellers to enter into small contracts including monthly, weekly, and even daily and hourly contracts. For buyers of hash rate, entering into smaller contracts helps control potential loss of real money as there is no way to know the value of the cryptocurrency a year from the investment date. Massive losses can be realized in real dollars by holding initial investments in cryptocurrency for long periods. NiceHash's mining platform allows buyers of hashing power to get in and get out fast. We will be using NiceHash as our example for setting up a cloud mining account later on in the "Getting in the game" chapter of the book. We will go over some of the basic steps to setting up a NiceHash account, funding the account with whatever coins, and buying or renting hashing power.

Cloud mining pros and cons

At closer look, there are a few advantages to choosing to mine in a cloud with a third party. First, there are very low startup costs involved. You can start with as low as twenty-five dollars to begin trying out the mining process on platforms like NiceHash. Cloud miners do not have to constantly monitor electricity costs at home. They do not have to sell mining equipment from a coin that may potentially become unprofitable to mine at home. For instance, Bitcoin became unprofitable for single miners at home due to the emergence of large mining farm corporations like Genesis Mining. Cloud miners do not have to deal with the equipment overheating and ventilation costs associated with running mining equipment at home. There are no bothersome noisy fans to deal with, and cloud miners don't have to deal with the pre-ordering mining hardware and waiting to see if manufacturers can fulfill orders on time to realize profits on coin mining.

With cloud mining platforms like NiceHash, you can choose to outbid other buyers and have the largest hashing power of the pool directed toward your mining agenda for the duration of your contract. Cloud mining on NiceHash is also beneficial if you know a particular coin that you want to put lots of hashing power into. You can do it quickly on NiceHash and stop quickly as well. Not only does NiceHash allow buyers of hashing power to create short-term contracts, it allows you to cancel your contract anytime during the duration and get your remaining funds back with no cancellation fees.

The disadvantages surrounding cloud mining with third parties are quite a few as well. Although not owning mining hardware can be an advantage, there is one disadvantage, which is usually realized in reduced long-term profits from outright ownership of the equipment. This is because once the return on investment (the initial price you paid to buy the hardware, setup running, and mining) is recovered; the rest of the money you make for the life of the equipment is all profit. Also, with cloud mining, you will pay out at least twenty five to thirty percent of your earnings in pool and transaction fees. Another disadvantage is that if the price of Bitcoin drops too low, the mining corporation can and sometimes will halt payouts or raise payout withdrawal thresholds. Your money can be tied up for up to a year or more with cloud mining companies that lock you into long yearly contracts. You can easily see the value of your initial fiat currency investment dwindling if the price of your chosen coin to mine starts dropping in fiat currency value. This becomes very frustrating to the buyer holding the contract who wishes to liquidate the remaining funds or earned funds to minimize losses. Also, there are numerous scam websites on the Internet that appear to be legitimate cloud mining operations but are simply not. They are outright swindles put in place to take your money. I personally lost a sizable amount of money with cloud mining scam websites. We will discuss the scams to look out for in depth in a later chapter.

CHAPTER 5

Mining pools and what to mine

Finding a mining pool

Most mining pools are specific to a coin and can be searched for using the coin name in Google. Finding a mining pool is an ongoing task. Most of your decisions to stay with a mining pool will be based on the profits earned during the time you are participating in that pool. Do your research on the mining pool you want to join. Since some mining pools can be more profitable at different times, it is important to re-evaluate your mining pools and find better ones weekly and monthly. There is a website called cryptocompare.com that lists most of the available mining pools today. The pools are ranked by number of stars on this website. There are however three main things to look out for when choosing a mining pool.

The first is fees charged. The fees charged can range from 0 to 10 percent or more and sometimes higher. Low fees can mean low pool earning power and low profits. Fees in a pool are lower if the miners are assuming the risk equally. The fees in a pool are higher if the mining pool operator is assuming the risk. Consider this when choosing your mining pool. Second, you want to look out for the country your pool is located in. Choose a pool closest to the country you are in. That would preferably be the country you're living in. It will allow you to earn the most money. Third would be the reputation of the mining pool. There are actually Bitcoin pirates lurking on the web trying to destroy the Bitcoin network. Do a quick search on Twitter to see if any negative information comes up on the pool that you are considering joining. Some well-known pools to avoid are the Antpool, F2toP pool, and BTC nuggets.

Mining Bitcoin in pools

Today, Bitcoin mining is mainly reserved for large mining farms. These farms are set up with thousands of high-end mining hardware. However, Bitcoin can still be mined at home with the right equipment along with Bitcoin mining pools. Yes, you can try to mine Bitcoin on your own, but mining is based on hashing power. When it comes to Bitcoin, most of the available mining applications and services run their own official mining pools. Unless you have 10 percent or more of the global hashing power available all to yourself, you will want to join a Bitcoin mining pool in order to mine Bitcoin profitably on your own. Using default mining pools are reliable because they tend to have several users and come ready with technical support to help you during your mining process. When a Bitcoin mining application or service is downloaded or activated on your device of choice, there will be a default mining pool available with it. You would only have to change from your default mining equipment to see if you can earn more in a pool when you want to. You are also able to change mining pools if you want to mine another currency within that pool. That is only if the pool supports mining more than one currency. Bitcoin mining pools support the SHA-

56 algorithm. Therefore, any cryptocurrency that is created using the SHA-56 script can also be mined within the Bitcoin mining pool. A few of the top Bitcoin mining pools are windows 10 Bitcoin miner application, Antpool, and Slush Pool. Just as a note, Slush Pool was the first Bitcoin mining pool created. However, it is no longer the largest Bitcoin mining pool.

SHA-256

SHA-256 is the algorithm that mines the famous Bitcoin cryptocurrency. However, novice miners may not know that SHA-256 mines multiple other coins. Mining non-Bitcoin currencies that the SHA-256 algorithm can also mine sometimes pays out more coins, and these coins can then be converted to the highly desired Bitcoin. Way more virtual cryptocurrencies can be named however, only a small number of algorithms mine all of those cryptocurrencies across the board. By now, SHA-256 script is probably the most popular algorithm that comes to mind when thinking of cryptocurrency. However, over forty cryptocurrency coins can be mined with the SHA-256 algorithm. Only a few are listed here: Bitcoin, Namecoin, Peercoin etc.

For a complete list, visit www.Bitcointalk.org. Although, in many cases, the bottom line profit earned per day is comparable for all the coins using the SHA-256 script, Bitcoin retains the highest US dollar value to date that uses the SHA-256 script. By the writing of this section however, the highest earning SHA-256 crypto coin is the Namecoin. Its blocked time payout interval is ten minutes. This is the same for Bitcoin. However, Namecoin's block reward is double that of Bitcoin with 25 coins paid per block versus Bitcoin's 12.5 coins paid out for a block to its miners in a pool. As you can see, many virtual currencies can be mined using SHA-256. The one that is the largest network and still worth the most money in any fiat currency on the SHA-256 platform is the Bitcoin.

Mining alternate coins

To be very clear, mining of alternate cryptocurrency coins is profitable but at another level. Cryptocurrency miners have multiple reasons for mining alternate coins only valued at two and three dollars. It may be said that because of the increased mining difficulty of Bitcoin, the yields from alternate coins are easier and fast adding up to what some believe to be more mining profit in the long run. Many cryptocurrency alternate coin miners enjoy mining lesser dollar value coins. The highest alternate coin value during the writing of this book is US$859.00. That is Ethereum. Ethereum is an alternate coin. Now, because most alternate coins are valued at only a fraction of the currency value of Bitcoin, you can expect to take quite some time getting a return on your investment mining alternate coins. We already discussed the increased startup cost involved in mining with GPU. However, many cryptocurrency alternate coin miners will be happy to tell you that they are mining at a profit, and that they enjoy mining their alternate coin cryptocurrencies.

Alternate coin algorithms

1. Dagger-Hashimoto mines Ethereum and Ethereum classic.
2. Cryptonight CPU mines Monero.
3. Scrypt mines Litecoin and Dogecoin.
4. ECDSA mines the Ripple.

I have only listed the top alternate coins trading on the top exchanges as of today. A website that will give you a comprehensive list of cryptocurrencies and their algorithms is listed here.

http://www.cryptomining24.net/list-of-cryptocurrencies

Only the ones that are quite popular and are of some value are the ones that I have listed here. Their algorithms can be found above. They are listed here for your ease of selection when activating your mining and contracts. Feel free to venture out on your own and find other cryptocurrencies to mine. I have only listed the ones that are currently earning money and increasing in value.

Although there are others, you will mainly be using the algorithms listed above to mine alternate coins whether you are mining at home from your own hardware, in a pool, or in a cloud. If you are mining alternate coins in a mining pool, it can be helpful to use a mining pool called "multi pool."This pool lets you know which coins to mine, and it will switch to the most profitable coin for your mining automatically. Mining alternate coins, as we discussed, is a miner solving transactions for any coin that does not use the SHA-256 algorithm. Mining of all alternate coins can still be done on a home PC with a reasonably powerful graphic card. As we discussed, all alternate coin cryptocurrencies must be mined on GPUs.

Remember, GPUs can only mine cryptocurrencies that application-integrated specific circuits cannot mine. Today, however, there is an application-specific integrated circuit available to mine Litecoin. And, as we know, Litecoin is an alternate coin. Some cryptocurrency miners find it quite lucrative to mine alternate cryptocurrency coins instead of actually mining Bitcoin. You can mine whichever alternate cryptocurrency you choose to mine. You can spend your cryptocurrency any way you want to spend it. Of course, you will only spend it with merchants who accept it as payment. The most widely accepted cryptocurrency by merchants to date is the Bitcoin. Most altcoin miners will want to convert their alternate coins to the highest valued coin like Bitcoin, Litecoin, or Ethereum. As with mining Bitcoin, miners can choose to mine solo or in a pool. If you mine solo, you will mine slower and may get a no coin reward up to the total reward for yourself. It makes much more sense to mine in a pool than to mine solo unless you own a good number of mining rigs to generate some serious hashing power on your own. Remember, once you have mined your cryptocurrencies, you will be ready to convert them to the fiat currency you want to spend it in. Otherwise, you will keep it held in the digital currency you have accumulated, and spend it with merchants who accept that currency.

Converting alternate coins and Bitcoins to cash.

At the end of the day, most people will want to convert the Bitcoin or alternate coin balance to the hard cash they are used to spending. This continues to be my favorite part of making the digital money. It transfers into real money. Feel free to do your own research on the currency exchanges you want to use to convert your virtual money into fiat money. Fees and speed of conversion will be a factor in your choice of course. Remember to use Google to find many conversion sites to assist you when deciding how many coins from one currency you will need to achieve a certain amount of coins in your desired currency. When converting currencies on exchanges, you will also be alerted most times when you have made some mistake. Paying attention to the number of zeros and the correct decimal places will be important steps to follow. Almost all cryptocurrency coins can be converted to Bitcoin. This is fine because Bitcoin is an acceptable method of payment in many locations now. Apparently, you can even pay for your coffee off your mobile device with a Bitcoin application called "Authy."

CHAPTER 6

Getting in the game, getting a wallet; no sweat

Wallets

You will want a wallet. How else are you going to store your digital money? A quick overview of wallets will show you the most convenient way to store your new crypto money. Of all the online wallets, only Coinbase offers 100 percent guaranteed protection for your funds in the form of Bitcoin, Bitcoin Cash, Ethereum, Litecoin, and US dollars. Coinbase is an online wallet as well as an online buying and selling exchange platform. Coinbase however, only provides these services for digital currency valued at hundreds of dollars or more. It does not manage coins worth only one or a few US dollars. It will be most beneficial to use a single online wallet that can interact with multiple blockchains. This allows you to manage more than one coin in a wallet at a time. Could you imagine holding a wallet for your $100 bills, a wallet for your $50 bills, a wallet for your $20 bills, and so on? It's just way too much trouble.

You can always choose to use online exchanges that don't accept US dollars. But I would look for a verification of identity link to your funds before processing. These types of verification identity links will be embedded in the websites. Online sites like Genesis Mining and Hashflare Mining use these identity verification links in place of accepting US dollars. However, they are not cryptocurrency exchanges. You will want to participate with an exchange that accepts and converts to traditional fiat currency. Why is this important? We will cover this in the details and the section called "Don't Get Burned out There." Most importantly, online exchanges operate as wallets also. You can expect to pay additional fees during currency conversions. The most popular currency exchanges are Coinbase, Gemini, Kraken, GDX, and CEX. 10.

Wallet safety

To really discuss wallet safety, we should talk briefly about the kinds of cryptocurrency wallets that are available to you. You will find there are three types of cryptocurrency wallets. The first kind of wallet is a software wallet. Software wallets are run on a mobile device, online, or on a PC desktop.

Desktop software wallets are a type of cryptocurrency wallet. Desktop wallets can only be installed on a desktop or PC and can only be accessed from that single device. These are one of the most highly secured wallets. Unless your PC gets a virus, you will be able to keep this wallet quite secure. You will need to keep a copy of your backup phrase in case your PC or desktop gets a virus, and your wallet is on recoverable.

Online wallets are also software wallets but they are accessible from anywhere and from any device. Why is that the case? It is because they are stored in the cloud. Online wallets are all controlled by third parties. Using online wallets will also mean having your private keys stored online. Online wallets offer the least amount of security for your cryptocurrency funds.

The last software wallet is the mobile cryptocurrency wallet. This type of cryptocurrency wallet is run on a mobile application on your handheld device. These wallets are quite handy to use at retailers that accept the cryptocurrencies directly. This wallet allows you to spend the cryptocurrency directly with the retailer without having to convert the cryptocurrency into fiat currency.

The next type of cryptocurrency wallets is called hardware wallets. Hardware wallets generally can support multiple currencies and software. They are small plug-in devices that allow you to make online transactions, and secure your data quickly. Hardware wallets can range anywhere from under $100.00 to well over $1,000.00. Although hardware wallets process transactions slower than online wallets, they allow you to maintain more control over your transactions. With these wallets, transactions are completed online. However, the storage of coins and private keys remain offline. These wallets provide some of the best security to your coins and private keys. If you do start using an online wallet exchange like Coinbase, you will want to eventually get an offline wallet. That offline wallet can be a hardware or a paper wallet. However, remember that Coinbase offers 100 percent guarantee on funds held in their exchange.

The last type of cryptocurrency wallet is the paper cryptocurrency wallet. Paper cryptocurrency wallets are hard to hack because they are not connected to the Internet. Paper cryptocurrency wallets are great wallets for securing large amounts of cryptocurrency. These wallets can be complicated to set up and tedious to use on a repeated basis. This is actually, what makes the wallets so secure and great for storing large amounts of cryptocurrency. To use this particular type of wallet, funds would have to initially be transferred to your paper wallet from a software wallet. If you want to use the funds again, you would just transfer the funds from the paper wallet back to your software wallet. You could then proceed with your transaction.

Why set up a Coinbase wallet?

Now that we are familiar with the kinds of cryptocurrency wallets that are available, let's see just how simple it is to set up a wallet. We will use an online-hosted exchange for our example. We are using Coinbase here because Coinbase is the only cryptocurrency wallet that provides

100 percent guarantee on funds deposited and exchanged through their platform. We are also using Coinbase because we can execute a few different coin conversions in this wallet and still be guaranteed on our funds should anything undesirable happen. There was a time when you didn't have to reveal your identity and when selling and buying using one of these wallets was completely anonymous. This is not the case anymore. You will need to authenticate your state issued ID or drivers license and provide a link to a valid bank account for your Coinbase wallet. These steps are necessary in order to set up your account properly and receive future money that you are going to make in digital currency. We talked about the two-step verifications. Coinbase will also take you through a series of two-step authenticating factors before you can buy and sell cryptocurrency on its platform. We will not be showing pictures of setting up a wallet here as we live in a tech savvy world where you can access a much better visual step-by-step guide by visiting a YouTube tutorial here: https://www.youtube.com/watch?v=zRm1SiQv_ow

Coinbase will still be one of the best wallets to have. Coinbase will convert your coins to cash and send them right to your bank account of choice. Coinbase has easy-to-use "buy" and "sell" buttons for access to your coins and quick ability to dump your coins. For setting up a wallet demonstration, you will simply create a wallet on the Coinbase.com website. You can also set up your Coinbase wallet on your mobile device. Simply enter your correct personal verification information, and enter your email address. You will receive a series of email verification codes and SMS verification codes. Enter your codes. Link your bank account. Then your Coinbase wallet will be ready to go.

CHAPTER 7

Time to buy Bitcoin off-chain and mainstream methods

To be honest, when I first started researching Bitcoin back in 2014, it was only hundreds of dollars for one coin. Even at that time, I thought, "Wow! Hundreds of dollars is a lot of money to spend for just one coin." Why in the world would I want to do that anyway? The truth is that you do not have to pay for an entire Bitcoin at once. You can purchase small increments or shares, as we've discussed, of the Bitcoin at different times. Multiple Bitcoin percentage purchases can lead up to acquiring a single Bitcoin. Let me tell you, even though I hold an undergraduate degree in finance, up until that point, I had never found an investment that would return so much money so quickly. I was immediately interested in acquiring Bitcoin. It wasn't until later that I learned about mining Bitcoin. However, in order to do anything with Bitcoin you have to get some Bitcoin. I have never purchased an entire Bitcoin at one time. Similarly, most of your initial transactions will be under the thousand dollar or even the hundred dollar mark when you begin purchasing shares.

We have already discussed wallets for cryptocurrency in the previous chapter. We will be referring back to Coinbase to learn how to make transactions from that wallet. We also referred to setting up a Coinbase wallet in the previous chapter. Now, when would you possibly want to buy Bitcoin? Maybe you would like to see how good you could do on a $50 mining contract from the comfort of your home on one of the acceptable cloud mining sites we referred to in the previous chapter?

We discussed a cloud mining platform named NiceHash. Since you do not own mining equipment or have lots of money, to begin research on how to make money in cryptocurrency, cloud mining will create a great option for you. We have also discussed the many benefits of cloud mining from the comfort of your home with NiceHash in the previous chapters. NiceHash has the best mining contracts with the best short-term expiring contracts.

We want our contracts to expire quickly when dealing with cryptocurrency because the price of cryptocurrency is extremely volatile. Remember, short-term contracts keep your money—your real fiat money that you have converted to digital money for the purpose of making more money instead of being locked up in a long-term contract that can turn unprofitable in a matter of days. I would rather lose money quickly over a short period and be allowed to dump in three days or less, if desired, than be locked in a contract that will have me continue to lose my money for multiple days as I watch the coin prices drop without being able to get out.

In some cases, people can lose their entire initial investment in addition to any gains they may have realized. This is enough to drive someone to madness. Just imagine watching your money go down the drain, and you are stuck in a contract. This is why I like mining short contracts in a cloud. The more attractive way to acquire Bitcoins is to simply mine them although this may be considered a slow route by some. That means making your own Bitcoins from scratch in a mining cloud or in the comfort of your own home.

Mainstream Bitcoin buying with Coinbase

Let's talk about Coinbase. Just about all cryptocurrencies can be bought and sold on online exchanges. Most even let you store your coins on their exchanges. The fact remains that it is considered unsafe to store your cryptocurrency funds in an online exchange. Furthermore, it is unsafe to store your fiat currency on an online exchange as well. Again, Coinbase is the exception.

So far, we have discussed the safest way to buy and sell only the top traded and top US dollar valued cryptocurrency coins on the market today. As discussed throughout the text, Coinbase is currently a wallet and an exchange of only the highest valued and trusted currency coins on the market today. Remember, Coinbase will require you to verify your identity. This is a great asset as they guarantee 100 percent of your funds stored on their platform.

Again, some cryptocurrency coins are just worth a fraction of a fiat currency. You will not find small valued coins on Coinbase. The Coinbase wallet and exchange has been the main focus of the wallet and exchange discussion. It is still advisable for you to do your own research, and take into account your level of risk assessment and your level of risk tolerance while conducting business with cryptocurrency. Consider these things while conducting business on cryptocurrency exchanges at all times.

Because Coinbase is so trusted, that trust helps fuel the volume of trades that backup the Coinbase exchange. What the backup does is that it adds a considerable amount of waiting time to your transaction confirmations. We have discussed confirmation transaction time and fees many times throughout the book.

There is a considerable amount of waiting time associated with buying coins through Coinbase's exchange wallet. Again, the upside of working with Coinbase is that your funds are 100 percent guaranteed on your transactions. However, I must share one transaction, which I was not too happy with. I understand this unfavorable situation is only a result of the backlog of the volume of trades that need to be confirmed in the blockchain, which means we need more miners, and the difficulty rate has to come down.

It goes like this. I had purchased Bitcoin at one price, and Coinbase held up the confirmation for that transaction for ten days. That was the standard reply from Coinbase on confirmations. Depending on volume backlog, you will wait three to ten days to have active funds in the currency you want. Now, within the ten-day period that my funds were held in limbo waiting to be confirmed by Bitcoin miners, I earned $958.62 in profit. This was due to the *rise in the coin price*.

At the time, Bitcoin was rising quite quickly and had been surging for a few weeks. I was so excited that I had earned close to $1000 in less than one week just by having some stake in Bitcoin from a recent purchase. Also, I had been watching the rise. However, my transaction was never confirmed during those ten days. Because there weren't enough Bitcoin miners to confirm my original Bitcoin purchase, that $958.62 profit never hit my Bitcoin balance, nor did it hit my US dollar bank account. In fact, as my luck would have it, Bitcoin's behavior at that time was to drop at least another five or six percent per day.

Bitcoin did actually drop quite low during the time my money was locked up waiting to be confirmed from the initial transaction on Coinbase.

I had decided to purchase $2500.00 worth of Bitcoin at the price of $10,100.00 per coin. Remember, you do not have to purchase an entire Bitcoin. I had been watching the trend, and Bitcoin was rising very nicely, peeking daily with earnings of about seventy to eighty sometimes over hundred bucks per day. My lucky self decided it's time to get in. I did not know I had just entered at the end of the uptrend, and that Bitcoin was headed down once again.

I purchased; my transaction was locked up for ten days, and I lost my mind as I gained $958.62. I had lost my money by the time my contract confirmed that Bitcoin had dropped to $10,054. I sold all shares but $30. If you look at the numbers, you will notice that I also lost a portion of my initial investment. Bitcoin has since dropped to lows of $7000. However, there is still money to be made. Despite losing the profit and a small portion of my initial investment, I like the fact that Coinbase had a sell button that I could push to immediately stop my loss. It also sent the remaining $2400.00 and some change back to my US bank account. It still took at least three days for the money to show up in my bank account, but my losses had ended.

Coinbase continues to be the wallet for me when I need to get my virtual coins converted to US dollars quickly and securely. This is only when I sell Bitcoin. I do not use Coinbase when I purchase Bitcoin because of my experience described earlier. I have learned that when buying Bitcoin, you want to purchase your Bitcoin, and have them available in your wallet as quickly as possible. This is so that you can begin earning as quickly as possible. Selling through Coinbase is very easy but purchasing Bitcoin and getting it to your wallet takes much longer through Coinbase, and I personally do not use Coinbase for purchasing any longer.

Hitting the track or off-chain transactions

I have expressed my frustration with the time it takes Coinbase to do a purchase transaction. So, instead of choosing a less secure exchange to buy Bitcoin and other Coinbase quality cryptocurrency, the other option is to buy locally, which is called peer-to-peer selling and buying, or sometimes it is called *off-chain transactions*. I personally have never had a bad experience buying locally with what's called off-chain transactions. For one, the transaction is confirmed much quicker. It is then entered into the blockchain forever just like every other transaction.

The local exchanges add a whole other dynamic to buying and selling cryptocurrency for users who do not want to wait for Coinbase or other large wallet exchange transaction confirmations. A seller would benefit greatly by selling on local exchanges because of the price increases that are allowed in the list price of your Bitcoin. The option of buying and selling locally is also only available for Coinbase quality coins right now. This is because of the high dollar value of the coins.

This type of coin trading called off-chain coin trading or peer-to-peer coin trading will require you to be a bit savvy in navigating exchange rates between the currencies you are working with. Making peer-to-peer transactions are easy. You are dealing with real people who own Bitcoins and want to sell directly to you. They are local to you as well. You have the option to buy across the world and the nation. However, it's easier to purchase and sell via locality due to availability of similar banks for your deposits.

When buying locally, you will need to look for the best exchange price for the type of transaction you are seeking. For instance, Bitcoin can be trading at the market value for $9500.00 in one second, but the cheapest US dollar exchange price you can find locally maybe $10,250.This will be frustrating. However, it is not a bidding war to buy Bitcoins on off-chain transactions. You just check the profile of the seller and the seller's reviews. If you like what you see, you open a trade with the seller. It is very easy.

Buying on the local exchanges can be compared to purchasing your last minute loaf of bread for breakfast toast from the gas station as opposed to purchasing it from Walmart or your regular food chain. We're talking about the pricing difference that you're going to pay. Buying Bitcoin with cash is most likely the quickest way to get your hands on some Bitcoin.

Reputable off-chain exchanges like your local exchanges have great escrow programs in place. These programs benefit both parties: the seller and the buyer. Once the trade is opened, the coins requested by the buyer are put into an escrow at the exchange until the transaction expires. Most trade contracts expire within four hours and must be completed and confirmed by both the seller and the buyer within that time or else nothing happens. This means that no Bitcoins will be transferred to the buyer, and the escrow will be released back to the seller.

I have had great experiences purchasing Bitcoins locally. The transfer of coins from the seller's wallet to the buyer's wallet happens in a matter of minutes in most cases. Many people prefer to be paid the Bitcoins they purchase in a matter of minutes rather than in a matter of days like with Coinbase. This is why I do not recommend Coinbase for the purchasing of any Bitcoins and only for selling Bitcoins directly to your bank account.

Buying Bitcoins off-chain through local exchanges

If you are one of those people who don't want to wait for Coinbase to take three to ten days to confirm your transaction, you will opt for a peer-to-peer off-chain purchase exchange. In my experience, buying Bitcoin and Litecoin locally is so much faster. This is very crucial when you are looking to jump in on a coin price increase trend. I don't discuss any of my investment strategies in this book, but I would say it is still not advisable to store your coin shares on these local exchanges despite their ease.

I always prefer to purchase from local Bitcoin exchanges when I need coins quickly. Coinbase will always give you the market value of the coin at the time you completed the sale; it will also give you the market value of the coin at the time of your purchase. Again, funds usually take three to ten days to confirm. The off-chain exchanges will also have buyers and sellers purchasing in current US dollar fiat money of your choice, but it will be at an inflated price because you want to purchase it now and have access to it within minutes not hours or days.

These local exchanges allow you to deal with local buyers and sellers by simply selecting the area closest to you to conduct local business. Deposits to pay for your coins can even be paid via Walmart to Walmart, PayPal, Federal credit union cash deposits, bank account cash deposit at the counter, person-to-person, Starbucks, or location choice transfers. Confirmations are required from both the seller and the buyer in order for the transactions to complete through these local exchanges.

Remember, a reputable local exchange has already taken your requested purchase amount of coins and placed it in an escrow account. The escrow is secure and held by the exchange. The coin will only be released to the buyer and removed from the seller's wallet if both the buyer and the seller complete their ends of the trade contract within the time allotted.

Buying exchanges like localBitcoins.com and litecoinlocal.com make it easy to conduct business with people. You can contact them quickly, and get your transactions processed within hours not days. Security is solid because it's very easy to receive or retrieve deposit receipts, and bank camera surveillance these days prove that you were somewhere depositing funds into someone's account. Of course, you would only do this in exchange for the owner of the account depositing Bitcoin into your wallet. Furthermore, transactions are not complete on these exchanges unless both buyer and seller confirm completion of tasks on their ends. Therefore, your money is protected, and you are protected because you're able to contact the authorities. Why? Because your transaction was in fiat currency, and fiat currency is regulated.

Local exchanges using escrows are safe for making coin purchases. I still encourage you to do your work, and read about the reviews of the sellers, and choose the closest locations to you. See how previous buyers have rated the sellers. Previous buyers will leave comments. The exchanges prompt buyers to do just that. Also, consider the duration of the coin release that is being reported for the seller after the seller has confirmed your payment, which is his or her requirement. You want a seller to have a very short coin release time preferably less than thirty minutes. Still your funds are in escrow, and it moves fast.

I have enjoyed dealing with local peer-to-peer sellers and buyers of Bitcoin and Litecoin. This is because I can make my cash deposits directly into sellers' bank accounts and receive my coins within minutes. My coin shares after the seller has confirmed my payment are usually released within minutes without delay. Beware that these purchase exchanges generally do not allow you to convert your currencies into other forms of coin. These are places to directly buy Bitcoin, Litecoin, and Ethereum. To convert your coins, you will need to send your coins from your local exchange wallet to your permanent transaction wallet whether that is Coinbase or an offline wallet.

CHAPTER 8

Converting currencies

Why do we need to convert cryptocurrency?

Converting cryptocurrency is nothing new. Anyone who travels knows they must exchange their money sometime or another. When you exchange the current type of money for a different type of money, you are converting currency. Another good reason to convert cryptocurrency is that it will turn your virtual money into hard cash that you can spend every day.

Another good reason is that you may want to changeover certain cryptocurrency coins between themselves—something like turning your balance of Litecoin to Ethereum. You can then cash out coins to cash in your personal bank account as well. Converting cryptocurrencies to other cryptocurrencies will become easier the more you do it. Generally, you will be working with only a few coins anyway. This is until you get good. I personally do not mine coins that are not of a high value. I am usually converting coins to cash most of the time. The coins that I convert are Etheruem, Litecoin, and Bitcoin of course.

I learned currency exchange during my undergraduate studies, but now it is very simple for everyone to do. There are multiple calculators for currency converters available on Google. If you do not know how to do any other currency conversions, you will want to know how to convert your coins to cash, and send them to your bank account wallet.

You will need to watch out for decimal places and the number of zeros as they mean large differences in the amount of money being sent and received. Do your conversions ahead of time on a piece of scrap paper. This is so you are sure about what you were sending, and what you are supposed to be getting in return. You don't want to miss on the coins and currency you're supposed to receive. The difference of adding or omitting one can mean pulling the difference of hundreds or thousands from your bank account or your wallet.

Converting cryptocurrencies to other cryptocurrencies or fiat currency requires IRS reporting of losses or capital gains. Something savvy crypto traders know to do is prolong the IRS capital gains reporting. This is done by simply keeping currencies within the digital realm. The gain or loss would go unreported or only be reported on the transaction that requires the use of fiat currency in the final conversion. This is an advanced technique, which I will not cover in this book.

You must however become familiar with the IRS section 1031. That section talks about these kinds of transactions. You will use those types of transaction reporting in the reporting of gains and losses of your cryptocurrency. Yes, there is real action here enough to make you emotional. Each person is responsible for his or her own reporting. To be candid, not all investors and traders actually comply with section 1031. It requires a lot of financial calculations and most just don't feel like dealing with them. Many just don't know how to do the calculations. As cryptocurrency becomes more regulated, so will its transactions. As of now, there are many moneymaking loopholes.

Handy currency converters or conversion example

The best way to convert currencies is to simply type the exact conversion information you are looking for in the Google search line. The main conversions you are going to be interested in are conversions from your current currencies to the cryptocurrency. You will want to know how to convert the cryptocurrency back to your current dollar as well.

We are going to do a simple conversion that you will need to know right from the beginning. We will be using US$50 for our example. Type the following line commands into the Google search line, and Google will tell you today's market value of the coin that you are searching for. The number you get today will be different from the numbers published in this book because these are the numbers of the market value of the coins on the day this example was created.

Convert US$50 to Bitcoin = 0.0072 Bitcoin
Convert US$50 to Litecoin =0.008449 Litecoin
Convert US$50 to Ethereum = 0.002322 Ethereum

Even though all the conversions ended in a fraction of a coin, they all equal US$50. Each one of the above virtual currencies can be converted into each other and into spendable cash to be spent at retailers.

Below is a list of some handy converters that I have saved to my home screen on my mobile device. This allows me to convert currency values and view them quickly at anytime.

Litecoin to US dollars
http://www.investing.com/crypto/litecoin/LTC – USD – converter

Bitcoin to US dollars
HTTP://www.unitconverters.net/currency/BTC-to-USD.htm

Ethereum to US dollars
Http://www.investing.com/crypto/Ethereum/ETH – USD – converter

CHAPTER 9

Don't get burned out there

It's important to highlight cryptocurrency scams so that people like you and I can stop being taken for our hard earned cash. There are currently five different types of cryptocurrency scams that are prevalent. All these scams amount to fraud, but some are more specific and frequent enough to be put into different categories of fraud. Claims that are general are classified as fraud claims and account for 30 percent of the cryptocurrency scams. There are cryptocurrency scams called exit scams. These account for 17 percent of the cryptocurrency coin scams. Phishing scams, which account for about 23 percent of cryptocurrency scams have been around for a long time.

Most people are familiar with the term phishing when it comes to emails and personal information being released online. However, we should not be surprised to see phishing scams show up in the cryptocurrency world. Scammers also use Twitter and Instagram to get people interested in potential scam websites. The largest phishing scams have both been at the two million dollar mark. Outright theft of the cryptocurrency coins account for another 17 percent of the scams.

The largest exit scam to date has been with Bitconnect exchange. The Bitconnect exchange exit scam was worth a whopping $250 million. The largest outright theft of Bitcoin was from a Russian developer who was beaten on the street and robbed of three hundred Bitcoin worth three million dollars.

We hear about coin hacks all the time and as large as the dollar amount sounds, hacks are still only accounting for 22 percent of the total scams in the cryptocurrency world. That always amazes me because losses are always in hundreds of thousands valued at hundreds of millions in currency value. With that being said, the largest amounts of money stolen continue to be during hacks. The largest reported coin hack was with Coincheck's $400 million during the first chance project hack.

Bitcoin phishing scams

Well, we know phishing to be some type of fake email from a supposed reputable company, which is really a fake company that is out to get our personal information, right? Phishing attacks are usually looking for the user's credentials, and their personal information in the advertisement. From what we know about phishing, we can understand that this type of scam is after the credentials that we use to access our cryptocurrency accounts.

Phishing in the crypto world is called *crypto phishing*. Some phishing scams have even begun to penetrate the Facebook community mimicking some of the Facebook layouts and tricking cryptocurrency users into entering their cryptocurrency information. This is a form of *crypto phishing*. Phishing scammers will create fake blockchain.infovariation to look like websites that cryptocurrency users are used to normally using. The scammers will then redirect cryptocurrency users to their own pages and have access to their cryptocurrency login information in wallet information.

Once an unsuspecting cryptocurrency user is on the cyber thief's site, and they proceed with their transaction as usual, the theft can take place from the phishing site. Most phishing scams empty your coins from the wallet address that you provide them during your transaction. A Coinhoarder campaign using Google Ad Words was unveiled as a phishing scam as recent as February 2018. The investigation showed the cyber thieves netting US$50 million in less than three years.

Phishing scam alerts to beware of:

- A text or email saying, "Someone just tried to access your account from another browser or IP address."
- Survey invitations about cryptocurrency events offering coins as compensation for your completion of the survey.

Avoid Bitcoin phishing scams by doing the following:

Avoid Facebook Bitcoin phishing scam by paying close attention to your privacy settings on Facebook.

Copy and paste links from emails directly into the web browser. Do not click links in your emails.

Invest in a phishing antivirus software free or otherwise.

Bitcoin hacking scams

It seems like at least every week we hear about a Bitcoin hack. Hacks of cryptocurrency happen mainly to companies like large exchanges. However, peer-to-peer hacking is possible at the simplest level. One of the worst peer-to-peer hacks happened to Apple's co-founder, Steve Wozniak. He made Bitcoins available for sale in an open market. His buyer was unchecked. The Apple co-founder finalized his sale and released his Bitcoin for whatever the sale price was. He had accepted payment for his Bitcoin via credit card. Well, his buyer canceled his credit card payment after receiving the Bitcoin. You see the bad thing about Bitcoins and any other cryptocurrency is that once it's released or sent, you can't get it back. There is no regulatory body that will go after your coins for you.

Some of the more sophisticated hack scams are executed through ICO (initial coin offering) pre-sales. If a hacker gets a hold of a list of interested ICO buyers, they can easily target them. These interested early buyers can end up sending their money to a fraudulent wallet address. This is what takes place at the beginning of any of these cryptocurrency coin launches. The largest virtual currency heist, probably in history, is the latest Japanese exchange Coincheck. Half billion dollars in virtual money was stolen. This very large hack happened just in 2018.

Ways to protect your virtual currency from getting hacked:

Mine your own virtual currency, and store your balances on a hardware wallet.

Do not store your virtual money on exchanges for any length of time. Do your exchanges quickly. Get in and get out.

Bitcoin exit scams

Generally an exit scam is a scam that consists of a fake company offering goods or returns on investments and then not paying or supplying those returns on investment after payment for such items have been received. In the virtual world, this can be executed during an ICO. This is when a coin is first introduced, and investors are recruited to financially back the coin.

Hefty gains on investments are promised to investors during ICOs with frequent, sometimes even daily, payouts to an account that you set up with the website, which is normally the exit scam website. These exit scam websites may payout returns for short periods, or they may have their payout thresholds extremely high so that no payouts can be requested. In the end, the exit scam website will disappear from the Internet with your funds; they will be unsearchable, and you will know that you have been scammed for your funds.

It is easy to be caught in an exit scam if the company paid you consistently for a while. You just expect things to continue as normal. However, one day, the company just stops paying, not only you but, everyone that has invested an account with them. The scammer has perhaps amassed enough money from the investors that they feel they can exit now with the money and not get caught.

This is just another scam that represents one of the top percentages of the different types of Bitcoin scams. So be very diligent if you are interested in ICOs. Check them out before you invest in them. I personally do not bother with ICOs due to the high risk of exit scams involved with them.

Free Bitcoins and faucet scams

I have never made any money on a Bitcoin faucet. I was scammed on quite a few of them though. The scam behind Bitcoin faucets is that most of the sites do not ever make the payouts that users are accumulating in their accounts. Your account or wallet must be maintained with the website, and your earnings, free earnings, or false earnings will be accumulated in that account.

The payout thresholds on the sites I used were so high that it takes so long for users to accumulate enough coins to request a withdrawal. They just give up before even requesting a payout. I certainly did. I didn't see the time value in visiting the site so much and winning so little. The amount of Bitcoin that they give you for free on the site is not worth your time. It's like getting the dust off a gold bar. You will need a lot of dust just to make one small piece of that gold bar. Your time and effort could be spent better elsewhere.

You may never get a payout from a free Bitcoin site. Bitcoin faucet sites are actually just put up to earn advertising fees from the banners that are listed on the sites. Bitcoin faucets do not intend to pay you free Bitcoin. There are even scams intricate enough on these Bitcoin faucets that when you win a specific amount of Bitcoin, you will supposedly have to send a separate miner's fee upfront in order to get your Bitcoin released. Of course, I tried this and got burned. My Bitcoins that were worth quite an amount of money at that time never got released to me. However, I had taken my American cash, converted it to Bitcoins, and paid the miner fee upfront in expectation of my Bitcoin that I had won. It was never paid to me. Bitcoin faucets are a scam. Do not waste your time with them.

In conclusion, Bitcoins are real, and there is real money to be made in limited ways none of which includes the word *free*. There is real money to be made mining Bitcoins and alternate coins. We have discussed the basic ways of mining that will generate income for you month after month after you have recouped the price of your equipment. Apart from a price rise upswing, this is the way to generate sustainable income from cryptocurrency.

This book did not discuss investment strategies involving cryptocurrency because this book is not written for the investor. Quite honestly, getting involved with cryptocurrency and making real, sustainable money in cryptocurrency does not require you to be investor savvy at all.

Yes, you can make some serious gains when the coin price is on the rise. However, the truth is that those upward swings don't last long. You must always be ready to dump. The most stable money strategy for obtaining cryptocurrency is mining it. You just need to know the truth about Bitcoin and alternate coins. I trust this book has provided clear insight into what Bitcoins and alternate coins are and are not. So forget all the hype. If you're mining Bitcoins, you will have a sustainable income that will continue to generate month after month. When the price of

Bitcoin coin rises, your income will rise with it, and when the price of the bitcoin falls, the income that you're generating from mining will drop as well.

However, there will be minimal risk involved with your mining. Moreover, remember that the creation of cryptocurrencies belong to the world. Cryptocurrency cannot be further created without a user and a miner. Miners are the ones that verify transactions that support these cryptocurrencies. Mining is for anyone and everyone. That's where the money is. There are no get rich quick roads with Bitcoin except for riding an upward price rising trend. So, get buying and get to mining. Have fun while you literally make your own money from scratch.

References:

https://Bitcoin.org/en/faq#who-created-Bitcoin

https://cryptocurrencyfacts.com/where-do-Bitcoins-come-from/

https://en.wikipedia.org/wiki/History_of_Bitcoin

https://www.ccn.com/altcoin/

https://blockgeeks.com/guides/litecoin/

http://fortune.com/2017/12/12/litecoin-Bitcoin-price-2018/

https://finance.yahoo.com/news/litecoin-everything-need-know-184858570.html

https://www.lifewire.com/cryptocoin-mining-for-beginners-2483064

https://www.youtube.com/watch?v=fNfr4bO5ElY

https://www.youtube.com/watch?v=YpJqibkPxBg

http://jkcrypto.com/NiceHash-review-pros-and-cons/

https://www.cryptocompare.com/mining/guides/#/overview

https://support.amd.com/en-us/kb-articles/Pages/Radeon-Software-Crimson-ReLive-Edition-Beta-for-Blockchain-Compute-Release-Notes.aspx

https://www.predictiveanalyticstoday.com/top-free-data-mining-software/

https://www.cryptocompare.com/mining/guides/how-to-mine-cryptocurrencies-without-a-mining-rig/

http://techglamour.com/cloud-mining-advantages-and-disadvantages/

http://jkcrypto.com/asic-mining-vs-gpu-mining/

http://www.tgdaily.com/cryptocurrency-and-blockchain/cloud-mining-vs-hardware-mining

https://Bitcointalk.org/index.php?topic=908441.0

https://ethereum.stackexchange.com/questions/26049/what-aspect-affects-the-gpus-mining-speed

http://cryptomining24.net/list-of-cryptocurrencies/

https://Bitcointalk.org/index.php?topic=1289689.0

https://www.reddit.com/r/Bitcoin/comments/7o0i9i/how_can_i_mine_Bitcoin_in_my_garage_that_has_no/

https://www.coinwarz.com/miningprofitability/sha-256

https://www.coindesk.com/cisco-50-million-Bitcoin-phishing-scam-mimicked-blockchain-web-wallet/

https://www.kaspersky.com/blog/crypto-phishing/20765/

https://www.forbes.com/sites/johnwasik/2018/01/31/how-to-spot-Bitcoin-crypto-scams/

https://www.nasdaq.com/article/what-is-an-ico-cm830484

https://en.wikipedia.org/wiki/Exit_scam

Glossary

Alternate coins (altcoins) - any cryptocurrency coins offered after the introduction of Bitcoin. All altcoins have a lower value than Bitcoin. Most altcoins claim to be a better version of Bitcoin. The highest valued altcoins are Litecoin and Ethereum.

Application-Specific Integrated Circuit (ASIC)-An application-specific integrated circuit (ASIC) is a kind of integrated circuit that is specially built for a specific application or purpose. ASIC can improve speed because it is specifically designed to do one thing, and it does this one thing well. It can also be made smaller and use less electricity. It can be used straight out of the box. ASICs mine only Bitcoin. Now, Litecoin specific ASICS are available.

Batch - a number of Bitcoin transactions bundled into one group by a Bitcoin processing platform in order to take up less space on the blockchain. Batching takes up less space on the blockchain thus decreasing transaction confirmation time. All Bitcoin transactions inside the batch must still be confirmed by miners.

Block - is a record of all prior cryptocurrency transactions that have not yet been entered in the blockchain as confirmed. Once the transactions are confirmed in the block, the cryptocurrency block will pay a cryptocurrency reward to the miners who solved that block of transactions. The block will then be recorded forever on the blockchain.

Blockchain -A blockchain, originally block chain, is a continuously growing list of records, called blocks, which are linked and secured using cryptography.

Coinbase - an online software cryptocurrency platform that provides cryptocurrency wallet and cryptocurrency buying and trading services. Coinbase is one of the most trusted online wallet platforms offering 100 percent guarantee for funds held and transacted on their platform.

Cryptocurrency -Cryptocurrency (or crypto currency) is a controversial digital asset designed to work as a medium of exchange that uses strong cryptography to secure financial transactions, control the creation of additional units, and verify the transfer of assets. It is a form of digital money.

Dump - to sell all or majority of your time investment in cryptocurrency. To press the "sell" button to sell all or most of your digital currency.

Fiat currency - any paper or coin currency that has no intrinsic value. This means the money is not backed by anything—no gold or silver. It is only money because the government says so. In 1971, Richard Nixon took the US dollar off the gold standard and devalued the American dollar to a worthless fiat currency.

Fork - a fork in a cryptocurrency is a positive change or upgrade to the computation process or mining process of the cryptocurrency. It makes the cryptocurrency easier to mine. It can be permanent or temporary.

General Processing Unit (GPU) - Graphics processing unit. These units are not able to operate independently. They do not mine Bitcoins effectively. These units are best used to mine alternate cryptocurrencies. You will need multiple GPUs to effectively mine any cryptocurrency.

Hardware wallet - is a type of cryptocurrency wallet that stores a user's crypto keys and cryptocurrency funds offline. This information is unavailable at all times until the user plugs the hardware wallet into an online device.

Hash power - unit of measurement of computing power consumed by any cryptocurrency in order for it to be continuously operable.

Hash rate - the most important data point in the blockchain's technology. It indicates how much power is being aimed at the blockchain from all over the world. Hashes are contained inside of a block.

Initial coin offering (ICO) - are similar to crowd funding in that the backers come from supporters for the new project. It differs from crowd funding in that backers of ICOs expect a return on their investment and supporters of crowd funding generally are donating and do not expect anything in return.

Miner - any person or entity that uses cryptography specific software to verify previous cryptocurrency transactions on a blockchain or within a batch of transactions on a blockchain. Anyone can be a cryptocurrency miner.

Mining farm - is a single location where a large number of servers and computers are all directed toward solving cryptographic equations that add to the cryptocurrency blockchains. Mining farms use more power than single miners.

Off-chain transactions - is a movement of cryptocurrency value outside of the blockchain. It is a way to bypass cryptocurrency transaction fees. This usually takes place through peer-to-peer transactions.

Software wallet - a software program that stores user's cryptocurrency keys and funds online. With this type of wallet, user cryptocurrency funds and keys are always online and available to hackers.

About the Author

Ms. Roze's interest was piqued by Bitcoin when the price was only $700. Ms. Roze was anxious to know the secrets behind the multiple newly found Bitcoin millionaires. With her undergraduate degree in finance and her low adversity to risk, Ms. Roze set out to get her hands on some of Bitcoin. She began buying and mining the coins. To her dismay, Ms. Roze lost over $3000.00 learning the ins and outs of making money with Bitcoin. She learned the ins and outs of Bitcoin and alternate coins through manual mining and cloud mining sites. She invested her own money despite the high risk due to the high payouts surrounding the currency. Today, she is able to share with you firsthand experience about navigating the cryptocurrency market including Bitcoin and other high valued alternate coins. She does this in plain English without all the confusing technical terms.